Death Ed. 101

Death Ed. 101

.

Death Ed. 101

101

SECOND EDITION

Death Ed. 101

Death Ed. 101

A Guide for
the Living & the Dying

SECOND EDITION

by: r. pasinski de

Death Ed. 101

10 9 8 7 6 5 4 3 2 1
Photography by r. pasinski
Copyright © 2014-16   r. pasinski
d. h. too productions   1602
ISBN-13: 978-1499737745
ISBN-10: 1499737742

DEDICATION

To all who have passed before us
To all who are in the here and now
To all who are coming tomorrow

LIFE:

NAKED IN

NAKED

OUT

CONTENTS

LIFE:
NAKED IN
NAKED
OUT

TO SEE

It Took Me
Awhile to See
I Didn't Know
How Long I Would Be

In A World
Where Death
Is Following Me

It Took Me A Long
Long While to See
I Didn't Know
How Long I Would Be

In A World
Where Death
Is Always
Following Me

LIFE:

NAKED IN

NAKED

OUT.

PREFACE

"A Guide for the Living & the Dying" It is a guide for all of us, for all sentient beings, all impermanent beings. A guide for all of us. Since all sentient beings, all people including you, me, and everyone we know and don't know are both living and dying at the same time. In all of us, new cells are being born, beginning life and old cells are decaying and dying. So in all of us, both processes are happening at the same time, all the time. Some parts of us are being born, and others are dying 24/7. It is only when individual cells or parts of our body decide to die at the same time or not form new cells etc. that we become concern about our life; concern about our death.

LIFE

NAKED IN

NAKED

OUT

HOW DO YOU LOOK AT QUIETUS?

There are four main ways most people handle Quietus; they choose to or not to, look at death: in ignorance, outside of their realm, academically, or in reality.

1. In Ignorance: Many people look the other way when death is on display. Many try to distance themselves from "it" by: ignoring "it," pretending "it" doesn't exist and "it" doesn't concern them. Some may even try to drink or drug it away; but that only moves them closer to their demise, the death they are attempting to run from and hide.

2. Outside of Their Realm: They enjoy seeing the

death of characters in books, movies and on TV (war, horror, mysteries, etc.) and sometimes in real life. Believing that death is something that happens to others or will happen to them: maybe! It is hard for them to imagine death will happen to them one day, and if it does happen, it'll happen to them somewhere in their distant, very distant future. Right now, it is something that's not important, not a concern, something not worth thinking about, or even discussing.

3. Academically: Most academics look at death from a distance, from the outside, from the physical aspects of death. (By dissecting the processes of death, the death of others, leads them to believe they understand all and everything about death and dying) From looking at the processes of death and dying of others and explaining all that leads up to it. Its history and its causes, from the different ways a person can die, to corpse preparation processes in various cultures, etc., etc., etc. It is all outside. There is almost no introspection, no soul-searching about one's life or imminent demise.

4. In Reality: Death as a reality of one's life. A Fact of Life. You were born and because of that factor, you will die. Moreover, looking at death

from the inside, looking out. Through introspection seeing how impermanent everything is, all of us are and using that impermanent factor for personal growth. Use it as a way of living, a way of understanding what's important in life, and in death; see how we need to live with and use both life and death as muses in our evolution.

• To face one's eventual demise, to look death in the eye and see that it is with all of us, all of the time: 24/7. It is like a shadow that follows us; it is with us no matter where we go or what we do. It is a shadow that exists, a shadow cast because of the light that is our life and as long as we have life's light lit, death will be its shadow. If you have an issue with death, it is because you are alive. Death is only a problem if you make it a problem.

• DEATH: WE CAN NOT LIVE WITHOUT IT •
• SO LET US TRY TO LIVE WITH IT •

Death: if we look hard enough at it, it will give us the ability to see, give us insight into life and death.
• To see how fragile our life is: in this world, in this environment. We are like the glowing filament in a light bulb. It is a bulb with only so

many hours to shine, within a fragile shell –our body- a shell that can break at any time; be broken long before its potential hours, its glowing filament has expired.

• To look at life's impermanent factor, our mortality and see that we are just human beings. One of numerous other sentient beings, impermanent beings on this planet, beings that have no need to cling, cling to ourselves or anything around us.

• To see how close we all are to becoming and one day will become just another cold and stiff corpse. A corpse our family, friends, and neighbors, maybe the academics too, can discuss over coffee. When we reach our L.A.P., -last animation point- when our form ceases to perform, and we are declared dead.

• To see that at the time of death the "3-B" process take hold. The first "B": The process of being "Bagged". It starts by being place in a large, black plastic bag for transport, from our L.A.P. (last animation point) to a boxing center aka mortuary. At the boxing station: the second "B" comes into play. The process of being "Boxed," being prepared and placed in a box aka casket/coffin for a short exhibition and when the display ends, the last "B" comes into play. The process of being buried or burned.

Death Ed. 101 looks at the fourth way. It looks at the reality of our life and our death. It focuses on our mortality, on our impermanence and on the impermanent world that surrounds us. It reminds us that we are a lot closer to our demise than we realize, a lot closer to leaving this world, this impermanent place, this temporary abode then we think. It makes clear that we need to embrace and enjoy this moment, this day, and every day before death comes into play and sweeps us forever away.

Enjoy The Day While It Last
Before it Turns into Your Past
Or Becomes Your Very, Very Last.

.

• • •

A SIMPLE GAME
Life Is a Simple Game
There Are No Winners
There Are No Losers
Everyone Comes Away from It,
Like They Came into It: Naked

LIFE: NAKED IN; NAKED OUT

E: NAKED IN

NAKED OUT

Chapter One

Impermanence

HUMAN BEINGS
- Impermanent Beings
  - Incessantly Clinging
    - Impermanent Things
      - •

What does it mean to be impermanent, to be mortal? It means that we are not here to stay; not permanent fixtures in this life we are just transient, and as a tourist, only leasing space, we own nothing. In this life, in this world, on this little ball, we do not have a permanent home. On this rotating speck of dust, we mistakenly call home and everything we cling to, attach ourselves to and can't live without, will one day be without us. It'll all disappear from our present world when we disappear from this world. Moreover, everything we cherish, loved, hated or were indifferent about will all be left behind for others to enjoy, embrace, get obsessed with and to treasure or hate until their expiration date comes around. Our time for all those so-called important things, important actives, all those impermanent things, all that impermanent stuff, will have passed, when we pass on. After we leave, the physical world will still be here with its sunrises and its sunsets, its rain and its snow, its heat and its cold. It'll still be there with all the people we knew and loved, and all the other people we never got to know and never will because it will be too late.

All of our worldly belongings, our family, our friends, our status and all our possessions and positions will be left behind. All those people we leave behind will still be doing what they do. We will be missed for a short while, then eventually forgotten, like all the other people we have forgotten after their passing.

All our possessions will become nothing to us when we change from an animated, living being to a cold and stiff corpse. Everything we owned will be distributed among our heirs with some – as we once called it- precious stuff ending up in the trash and still other stuff at a garage or estate sale.

Who knows when all those we leave behind, will follow in our footsteps after we go? They too are impermanent beings, clinging to impermanent things and will one day follow in the footsteps of all the other impermanent beings that have passed before them. When death arrives at their side and cries: your life is up, it is time to go, don't pack anything, you'll be traveling all alone, my departing soul. That is when all the stuff they loved and cherished so, will be like melting snow, flowing toward the drain, back into the sea, into the sea of life from which it came.

Mortality, in general, is not something we usually look at, and our mortality is something we see even less, possibly because clouds aka the hustle and bustle of life shroud our consciousness. We live in a mirage, a dreamlike state, in a surreal world. We follow the dreams thrown at us from birth by our parents, our siblings, our peers, the media, its ad agencies and so-called news organizations. Thereby not realizing what life is, never realizing that we are temporal things, mortal beings, with impermanent flings and have no need to cling and need to remember too, that we could be plucked out of this life at any moment, at any time, at any place.

There are times when our mortality does rise above the clouds, to the surface of our consciousness and suddenly shows itself, somewhat like a Jack-in-a-Box that pops his head out of its box and surprises us.

This conscious awareness of our mortality could happen if, like Jack, Jack in the Box, we pop our head out of our dreamlike state and look past the mirage. When a surprise death happens, a sudden death situation occurs, and it happens to be someone we knew or loved. The closer we were to that passing-person, the more we are surprised, shocked and devastated, the better, the chance our head will pop out, look above the clouds of delusion and connect the dots. The dots if you connect them, are the same for all of us, they start at our birth, pass thru a segment of time and ends with our demise.

However, more than likely we will not connect the dots, we will not connect our humanity with the mortality of the person whose sudden death just occurred, the surprise death that showed us impermanence in action. If that connection does not happen, and we do not see the light from that incident, then all is forgotten. It is like when we close the lid of Jack's box, and Jack goes back into his dark, empty box, and we never see Jack again. Thus, if we do not see the light, the awareness of our transience it will go back to its buried ground in our subconscious and our dreamlike, delusional state will start up again. It'll continue until another surprise death occurs, and Jack again pops out of his box, and our mortality again stares us in the face.

Most of us never look at our mortality because we fear death and see it as something that is going to take away everything we hold dear, including ourselves and we, don't want to let go of any of it. Especially ourselves. We have this fear because no one told as a child that we were impermanent beings and that death was just a part of our new life because we are mortal beings. Being born was the first part of our journey through this life, through this transience life and dying is the last part, the end of that same voyage, that same life; life and death are twins. We are born with both, and both follow us through life, but death always wins in the end.

Life and Death are like Siamese twins and all sentient beings come with a pair; both twins are needed to move us efficiently, and successfully through life with harmony and understanding.

Life gives us mobility and leads us thru life and to our impending demise. Death gives us direction and keeps us in check. Our Life can get out of control, and we could lose our bearings and start attaching ourselves to things if we forget the most important part of our life: our eventual demise.

Death besides having the ability to close our life also can heighten our life; it can give our life light if we follow its directions. It is there to reminds us; it whispers in our inner ear every day: remember me, remember you are mortal, remember you are just an impermanent being. Remember, you have no need to cling, cling, cling to all those shiny, worldly, impermanent things because they are just like you, a passing fancy and in time will go when it is time for me to come by and say: Hello!

Wake up! Wake up! Wake up impermanent being!

Before it is too late. Do not, do not, do not cling, cling, cling!

Can you hear what death is saying? Remember my friend, you came into this life with nothing, and you will leave it with nothing.

LIFE: NAKED IN: NAKED OUT

ARE YOU TRAPPED IN YOUR TRAPPINGS?

Need help, detaching the self from life's trapping?

Maybe by looking into what it might be like being a corpse in a coffin (see PDE Chapter 13), we could see life's trapping for what they really are: just empty vessels. We could also connect with all of our events; one's missed because we postponed them (regrets), observed events completed and one's we are planning. It could be a good time to check our bucket list too. What do we want to do before we die and are we moving toward that goal?

Maybe you wish to look at the impermanence of all and everything in life and see it all from the perspective of a corpse in a coffin. Remembering that one day, we'll all be one: just another body in a coffin with a headstone at our head and a mound over our final bed.

A CORPSE IN A COFFIN

A Corpse in a Coffin
It's Our Future You See
A Corpse in a Coffin
One Day We Will Be
A Corpse in a Coffin
You & Me

Our Greatest Teacher

Our death besides taking our life, in the end, has the potential to enhance our life, in the here and now. It can be our greatest teacher, a mentor in this life if we open up to it. A teacher that is with us constantly, a teacher that is with us: all the time, 24/7, every day, every moment. Whispering in our inner ear, if we are open to it, reminding us that we are mortal and not a permanent thing, but an impermanent being, a being with no need to cling, since we live in an impermanent world. It is a world filled with other impermanent beings and things. It is just a figment, a fabrication of all those other impermanent things that surround us every day. So why cling? It is best just to remember you are a transient being, a tourist, a part-time boarder, no more, no less.

Our job is just to observe, to watch over our self, the environment, our movement and the movement of all those other impermanent beings and things that surround us every day, but to remember always not to cling. Enjoy them, interact with them while you can, cuz they are all just passing fancies and like you and me: in time will go.

Impermanent

Being

CLINGING

Impermanent

Things

Chapter Two

Naked In

We come into this world naked, with no coverings, no titles, no possessions as a small child, a naked child with a blank slate: morally, mentality and physically naked. We come without shame of our nakedness, having no idea what shame is, having no idea what anything is, or what coming next. What's coming next for most of us is accumulation. We start accumulating: stuff and more stuff, and still more stuff.

We soon start developing ideas, ideas about this, ideas about that, we are beginning to shape our new world, and one of the primary shapers of this new world is our accumulations. Our collecting continues to grow with the addition of feeling. Feeling with emotions, follow by gathering, collecting, taking positions and finishing with defending those feelings, those positions, those possessions and all those accumulations. Our world is taking shape, and we are starting to cling to it all, attach ourselves to it all and identify with it all.

Most humans in their early years learn about Santa, the bearer of gifts. Someone we learn to love and look forward to seeing every year because we know he'll bring us everything we want, and we've learned to want stuff, lots of stuff. Soon we slowly find out that Santa is not real, he is only a myth. So when Santa begins to lose its appeal, or we realize there's no Santa, and there's no more free stuff; our parents were lying to us, lying to us all that time. Our dream is gone, and we may feel empty inside.

Soon after, if not before, we find out about sex, something else our parents may have kept from us. The problems started early. From their lies about Santa to their secrecy about sex, most parents do not tell their children much of anything about: what's real, what underlies their lives, their existence. From Santa to sex, to the most important part of their life, the part that will one day take them and everyone they know away, take them all back. Back to the land from which they came, back to the land of nonexistence.

Most parents neglect to tell their offspring one of the most crucial and pivotal facts of their life. The fact that they are mortal, and this life, this life there in right now, this life they are embarking on would one day terminate. It would end with their demise, and that death could happen at any time and any place during their life's journey and we being their parents, have the same fate: we too will perish one day.

We need to remember that no matter what path we choose or not choose we'll all end at the same place. The path our parents took, the path we chose ourselves or the road we just stumbled upon whatever path we decide to take, or not take, we'll all end up at the same place. The place that all journeys do when they end, at DD's: Death's Door.

CHOICES

No Matter What Kind of Life

We Choose

Or Not Choose

Or Can't Choose

We'll All End Up in A Place

We Don't Choose

Death's Place

We need to remember that no matter how many accolades, titles, dollars, and possessions we've accumulated over the years or how much cash we have stashed in the bank, nothing will help us; in the end. Nothing will be coming with us; nothing will help us in the end, at our end.

If we only knew at the beginning of our life while we were still young, that you, me, our parents, our friends, and all the other numerous sentient beings on this planet where mortal. Maybe then we would not have tried to cling to, attach ourselves to or held on so tightly to: our self and our accumulations thus believing we would have them forever. If only!

"Somebody should tell us, right at the start of our lives, that we are dying. Then we might live our life to the limit, every minute of every day. "Do it! I say. Whatever you want to do, do it now! There are only so many tomorrows.

"Pope Paul VI (1897-1978)

IF ONLY

• If only they told us about death at the time, they taught us to read and write or at the time they told us about sex.

• If only they told us: that death was the great equalizer in life and that death is in everybody's future. • If only they told us that: no one would miss out on the death experience, no one will escape it, not the richest of the rich or the poorest of the poor.

• If only they told us: that since we were born, we are going to die, that our birth certificate is our guarantee to die certificate too.

• If only they showed us: that death is the great equalizer and that we are all equal in the eyes of this great equalizer: death.

• If only they told us that death, outside of taking our life can also enhance life. Enhance it by letting it be our guide, our muse, by letting it escort us thru life. If we let it in, it can be our greatest mentor since it is always with us, with us 24/7 reminding us: not to cling to impermanent things. However, to enjoy the day while it last, before it turns into our past, or it becomes our very last.

• If only they told us the real facts of life, the facts of life and death, early in life.

THE WINNER

After All Is Said & Done

Death Wins Over Everyone

If only they told us the real facts of life and death early in life, that information alone could've sent our lives down a whole different path. A path toward equality, toward seeing the equality of all sentient beings and not toward our clinging, our continuous accumulation of impermanent stuff, but in a different direction, a direction towards a balanced life. By seeing the equality of life and not try to separate or raise, ourselves above or see ourselves as less than others, but to see ourselves and the rest of humanity as equal. Just see ourselves as Simple Human Beings no more, no less. Being the same, the same as all the other people on this planet and like everyone else in this world. We all have the same fate; we'll all go through the same life cycle of being born, living a short while, and dying. The same life cycle that every other sentient beings on this planet goes through with lives that are part-time, transient, impermanent. The fact that one-day, we'll be gone, we would cease to exist and us humans, being the biggest accumulators, the most prominent cling-ons on this planet, would lose the most. We would lose everything we've gathered, collected and cherished. Everything, our family, our friends, our status, everything we've accumulated, amassed, everything we've clung to, and everybody we know and love. I'll all come to an end when our life comes to its end.

A SIMPLE GAME

Life Is a Simple Game

There Are No Winners

There Are No Losers

Everyone Comes Away from It,

Like They Came into It: Naked

• LIFE: NAKED IN; NAKED OUT •

Life is a simple experience if we inwardly let go of its trappings and see ourselves as just Simple Human Beings, no more, no less. With the knowledge that in the end, like in the beginning, we will all be naked again and one day, we will all return to the land of nonexistence.
NAKED OUT

THE PROBLEM
THE PROBLEM
THE PROBLEM

THE PROBLEM

The Problem Started
When We Were Born
Our Folks Never Stated
One-Day They
One-Day We
Would Be Gone.

Has anyone ever told you about death? Do you remember how old you were when you first realized you were going to die and that your death is somewhere in your future? Do you still not realize it? Still not realize that you're a transient, a tourist, that you're just a visitor?

They told us about Santa except that he was fictional, little about sex and nothing about death. They told us nothing probably because our parents were uncomfortable talking to us, or thinking about both sex and death, probably because with their parents, our grandparents, those subjects were taboo too.

If you are a parent, are you going to keep silent like your parents or grandparents did or:

• Are you going to break the ice?

• Are you going to tell your children that you, they and everyone else they know are mortal and will one day die?

• Are you going to tell them that everything in this world is impermanent?

• Are you going to tell your children that you are going to die one day too? • Are you going to tell them that they are going to die one day and that day is somewhere in their future?

• Are you going to tell them anything about impermanence, anything about death?

Alternatively, are you going to keep silent and keep death in the shadows?

If no one has ever told you about death, I guess now is a good time. A good time to let you know, to let you know: you are not permanent; your life is only a part-time position. One day, it could even be later today or maybe tomorrow, or next week, or next year, you'll be fired; your life expired.

One day you are going to die and be called back to the land of nonexistence. Yes, you! That person you see every morning in the mirror. You, you, you!

MIRROR
Mirror, mirror
on the wall
One Day
   my image
     my form
       my life
         will be
           No More

You Won't Need
Your Purse
In Your Hearse

THE CASH & THE CRASH

All of Our Accolades

All of Our Cash

Everything We Know

Will One Day Crash

Our

Siamese

Twins

Chapter Three

Our Siamese Twins

TIME
Today's time
Enjoy it while it last
Before it turns into your past
or becomes your very, very last

IT'S TIME TO ENJOY LIFE

Now's the time to enjoy life: to get more joy from life, from the day, from the moment. Now's the time to reconnect your twins, your Siamese twins "L" and "D," the twins that have been with you, at your side since birth.

Most of us have been loving one twin and ignoring the other and thus keeping them apart, apart for far too long. Our Siamese twins are our twin "L" (life) and our twin "D" (death). We've been accepting one twin "L" (life) and ignoring, tuning-out, brushing off the other twin "D" (death) for far too long. Our twin "D" (death) isn't something to ignore or dread, but something to be aware of, to be conscious of, something to embrace. Embrace it because in life, there is death, and in death, there can be life. They are Siamese twins that can't be separated. If we keep them apart, we'll end up living half a life. Our Siamese twins are our life and our death, and they both go together like a horse and carriage, we cannot separate them, we cannot have one without the other. However hard we try, and we are trying hard, we are working very, very hard to separate our twins, to keep them apart. We need to Stop, stop trying, we need to Stop ignoring twin "D" (death) and bring "D" back into our life.

We need both twins working together for a well-balanced, harmonious life. The twin "L" (life) gives us movement, but can get out of control and lost; it can start to cling and accumulate.

Twin "D" (death) helps keep us on track, keeps our life in order. It gives us direction and insight about our form, our movement, our environment and our life. It shows us the way: it shows us how to live a cling-free life.

DEATH

• It reminds us that we are not here to stay.

• It reminds us that we are all impermanent beings, living with impermanent things, in an impermanent world.

• It reminds us that we are only here for a short period of linear time. So we need to embrace, cherish and look at that time. We need to watch the clock and not waste our precious time amassing, accumulating, and thereby attaching ourselves to the physical, the material and the intangibles in this world.

Our Siamese twins are like an extra set of eyes and we need both of them working together to live a full and balanced life. If one eye is closed, we are only living half a life.

We need our twin "D" (death) to give us direction. To reminds us: we are not here to stay, we are not here to accumulate or cling, we are here to be free, to be free of all of that clinging, all that accumulation. Our twin "D" (death) can be like our personal muse. Showing us that everything is irrelevant, irrelevant not in itself, but to our impermanent existence, to our impermanent world, to our limited life. Irrelevant to the fact that nothing comes with us at our end, not our body, not our family, not our friends, not our accumulations. Nothing is coming with us when our life ends. We need to let our twin "D" (death) in. Let it in to show us the way, show us that we need to enjoy the moment, the day, today, each and every day before they're all swept away.

Are you ready to smell the roses along the way? Ready to smell: not only the roses but also all the other flowers along the way, along the way to your final day? Then let's start experiencing them today, it is the only way before we pass away.

WORRIED?
Worried About Losing Everything?
DO NOT!
One Day Everything Will Lose You.

One Day

One Day It'll Happen
One-Day Death Will Come By
Come by & Say: Hi
It's Time to Wake Up, My Friend!
It's Time to Come to My Den.

Memento

Mori

Chapter Four

Memento Mori

- Remember Your Mortality
  - Remember You Must Die
    - Remember You Will Die

We quickly forget that we are all mortal, and we are all going to die one day. Our society is geared to repress that fact and keep us from realizing: we will not live forever. They sweep up tragedy so fast and move us away from it even more quickly.

Are you ready to die? It sounds like a threat, but it is a condition, a condition of realization, a recognition that we cannot escape death. Thereby accepting it as part of our life and with that acceptance we've distance ourselves from all our accumulations.

• • •

We need to always remember that our demise can arise at any time and pluck us out of life. We are like feathers on a chicken's back, and when a feather is plucked the chicken survives, and it goes on with its life. The feather not missed, and a short time later, if not at the time it is plucked, the other feathers fill in that space and the chicken goes on until another feather plucked. So we need to be ready and not be surprised when death arrives at our side and plucks us out of this life.

An excellent way to remember and focus on your mortality is with this book, but it may not be enough. Just reading about death and one's mortality is a good start. However, after we put the book down our mortality may slip away and become secondary to whatever we are currently doing and in time, our impermanent factor can get buried again under all our other activities. We need to keep our mortality on the surface, where we can look into it: two, three, maybe four times a day. Set aside time and a place where you can be mindful of your situation, your place in life and the possibly of a surprise death. Meditation is an excellent way of becoming aware of life and death.

A good place to focus on our mortality is at Wakes aka funerals. It is a great place to see impermanence-in-action and peek at our future.

We need to look at the deceased in their coffin and remember one day we'll be there as the guest of honor, one day we'll occupy that space in our coffin as others fill the other spaces as descendants or friends at our Wake, as our body moves along to its final resting place.

Another great way to remember your mortality is to read a chapter of DE 101. It would be great if you could read a chapter every day or every week. The more you read it, the more you'll come to understand your relationship between life and death.

Still another great way to see impermanence-in-action is with surprise deaths.

I focus on my mortality daily by reminding myself every morning that this could be the beginning of the last day of my life. By the end of the day, I could be dead.

Many people will wake up today or tomorrow; a

lot woke up yesterday not expecting to die. To die on that day and will be surprised when they do or were surprised when they did; if they had, or will have time to be surprised.

Do you want to be prepared or surprised when your demise arrives? It is up to you. Death will come by one day; that is no lie.

OUR LIMITS
Death Will Come
To Most of Us
When We Least Expect It
And to All of Us in The End.
Our Limited Time
Our Limited Life
Will Then End

PLANS
Make Your Plans
But Keep in Mind
That You Can Die
At Any Time

"Life is just a short walk from the cradle to the grave, and it sure behooves us to be kind to one another along the way."

A. Childress (1916-1994)

Surprise

Demise

Surprise

Chapter Five

The Surprise Demise

THE PROBLEM
The Problem Started
When We Were Born.
Our Folks Never Stated:
One-Day They
One-Day We
Would Be Gone.

Do you like surprises?

Almost everybody likes surprises, but there are some surprises that most people dread, and one is the Surprise Demise.

There are two types of Surprise Deaths.

The first surprise death is the occurrence surprise death; where will our demise take place. Most of us would like it to occur in our sleep at night, thereby waking up dead in the morning, but that happens to very few.

The second surprise is the surprise demise we need to get away from, to eradicate, that is the shock of a death ours or anybody else's demise happening when it does, thereby not being ready to accept it as a part of life or being traumatize by it when it does happen.

We need to remember that, in the next twenty-four hours or less, someone's death could occur, and you, I, or anybody we know could end up being no more, and we always need to be ready to accept that demise and not be surprised by it.

Almost everybody likes surprises, but there are some surprises most people dread. Every day you'll find them, those numerous surprises on your smartphone, on TV and in the daily news; every day you'll find a surprise or two, sometimes three or more in the media, a surprise that some people ignored while others are deeply moved by, upset by and sometimes shocked. Shocked when they see or hear the news about somebody they knew either personally or were a fan of, had died. Surprise deaths! Will you be prepared or surprised when death arrives?

Recent surprise deaths of celebrates that covered the news and stunned their fans include: "Sopranos" Star: James Gandolfini, "Glee" Star: Cory Monteith, "Fast and Furious Star: Paul Walker and comedian Robin Williams.

Why are most people surprised or stunned when death arrives? They are surprised because they were not ready for those deaths. Not prepared for that person or those people to die at that time but somewhere else in their future, if they were prepared for death at all, theirs or anybody else's. They, like most of us, were never told about death, what it is and what it can do, when we were young.

If death were like birth, we would have nine months to prepare for it, but it is not, death's arrival can take a lot less time; it can happen in less than nine seconds.

Are you prepared for its arrival? How much time do you think you'll have to prepare for death? We'll have as much time to prepare for death, as we have to live. Think about it! We can start preparing for our demise and the death of others right now. By realizing that there was a time when we did not exist, and they did not exist, and there will be a time when we will not, and they will not exist again. Remembering that we came from nonexistence into existence when we were born and when our demise arrives, we'll transfer back from existence to nonexistence. Reflecting on our eventual demise is a good way to start preparing for our next transferal, the time we go from existing back to not existing. If we start now, we may be ready, be prepared when death finally arrives.

We look at these sudden, surprise deaths in the news and relate to some and ignore others. Most of the sudden, surprise deaths in and out of current-day news take most people by surprise: the deceased as well as their descendants, friends, neighbors, fans, and acquaintances.

Most unexpected, surprise deaths like sudden organ failure or an accident, etc. are usually a surprise for the deceased moments before the incident. Surprised because they never expected to die at that time; they woke up that morning not expecting to die that day, never expecting that day to be their last. They had a whole to-do list of other so-called "important things" they wanted to do, they wanted to accomplish that day and to die wasn't on that list.

That is a surprise death: a death that's never expected or planned. A demise that the deceased, as well as their descendants never thought would happen when it did, but somewhere else in their future. If the deceased or their descendants had ever thought about how or when they or people, they knew would die.

If they were not in a place, where they were ready to die. A condition where they had let go of life by cleaning up and keeping clean their relationship, with everything inside and outside of it. They would not have been surprised, but prepared for their death day. The day they would die because they had accepted death as a natural process and knew it could happen at any time and any place. So they did not leave behind: unfinished business, unfinished business with their family, their friends or foes. Leave behind any business that could form regrets about the deceased or its death that could follow their family, friends, and acquaintances to their grave

Almost two million people die every year in the U.S., and most of them are surprise deaths with nearly ninety thousand dying from alcohol-related events, over thirty thousand dying from gun-related incidents, and around thirty-five thousand people die in car accidents and almost all of them are surprised deaths. That is over 2900 car-related deaths a month from car accidents, over 670 deaths a week, over 95 deaths a day, close to 2 people dying every day, in every U.S. state, in car accidents.

In China alone over 200,000 people die in car accidents every year with many more people dying in other sudden-death situations. It means that a majority of these people started their day never expecting their demise to arise when they did and were surprised when it did surface if they had time to be surprised. Their friends and family probably were shocked too and now have to live with the circumstances. Live with what just happened; be alone with their unfinished business –if any- with the deceased, business that will remain forever uncompleted.

Regrets, regrets, regrets! However, they did not have to be surprised; they could've been prepared, ready for that death, ready for any death and not been left behind with sorrow and regret.

Is there anybody, anybody you know, if they died today would generate regrets in you, your family or friends psyche?

• TAKING NOTE •

Noticing surprise-deaths is another great way to see impermanence-in-action and to remind yourself that you are impermanent too and that your death could happen at any time. Noticing the surprise deaths of other impermanent beings, like yourself, happening every day via the media and in your life; you'll see how high the number is, of daily surprise deaths. These deaths not only occur in car accidents, hospital stays, and sudden medical conditions but with some very unusual freaky accidents too. See examples below:

EXAMPLE: A young couple with their 18-month-old baby from Washington State was driving under an overpass when a large chunk of concrete fell on their car, killing the trio.

EXAMPLE: A father and daughter on holiday with their family were walking along the shoreline on a beach when a small plane had to make an emergency landing on that beach. The pilot did not see the pair and the father and daughter died.

EXAMPLE: After leaving their wedding, a couple stopped to help a motorist on an expressway and were both killed when struck by another oncoming car.

EXAMPLE: A young man was walking on a boardwalk on a California beach on a bright sunny day when some dark clouds suddenly appeared, a bolt lighting struck the man, and he died.

EXAMPLE: On the East Coast, a young TV actress was riding her bicycle in the park when a tree uprooted by a recent storm fell on her.

EXAMPLE: In the Midwest, a lady was walking along a city street when a gargoyle broke loose, from a building and fell to the street thereby killing her.

• • •

All surprise deaths that happen, though tragic, can be excellent reminders, reminding us that by not preparing we too could one day be a surprise death, to someone, including ourselves. All deaths, especially surprise-deaths are a reminder that we are not here to stay. However, we are just one of many visitors, visiting other guests. It is like we are living in a large hotel, and we are all guest. Some of us with longer stays than others, but all of us having to check out one day.
Have you noticed anyone checking out, any surprise deaths lately?

ANY TIME

One's Demise Can Arise

At Any Time:

In The Morning

In The Afternoon

Or at Dinnertime

PLANS
Make Your Plans
But Keep in Mind
That You Can Die
At Any Time

Chapter Six

Sorrow & Regret
Regret & Sorrow

HOW ARE YOU
SPENDING THE DAY?

How Are You Spending the Day?
The Day That Could Sweep You Away
Are You Wallowing in Regret?
Or Enjoying What Time May Be Left?

We started being sorry a very long time ago; most of us cannot remember our first feeling of sorrow. Many of us learned about being sorry from books; read to us as a child. We saw in those numerous stories, how the characters, under certain conditions, generated sorrow for their actions. It showed us that we needed to produce sorrow too, if similar events occur in our life, and soon being-sorry became a condition, a condition in our life. Conditions where we had to: under certain circumstances evoke sorrow. We then added other things we thought we had to be sorry about, and that list grew over the years.

Did those feeling of sorrow come from missing out on something or were we told, we needed, to feel sorrow because of something we said, or did, or something that just happen?

Over the years, most of us find that our sorrows could metamorphose into regrets, and these regrets could grow and last a lot longer.

Most of our regrets are sorrows that have moved from a small temporary position to powerful, long-lasting position. Shallow sorrows are usually small and may last from a couple of minutes to a week, whereas regrets have a much longer lifespan. Some regrets live as long as we do and become our lifelong companions. They cling to us like blood sucking vermin. We sometimes unconsciously cling to them by funding them, by feeding them. We nourish them with our generation of thoughts, repeated thoughts about an incident that happened yesterday, an incident that caused the regret to form, to take its shape. Over time, this monster will grow and grow if we feed it with our incessant thoughts and can become a companion, a hardened part of our inner life with the possibility of it expanding into our outer life over time if we do not nip it in the bud.

These types of regrets are like ugly green monsters and may plague, torment and traumatize us for years, destroy our life and follow us to our grave. Do we want these ugly green monsters on our back every day, stalking us, dragging us down, destroying our life? I believe most of us do not.

It is best to avoid these ugly green things if we can and get our regret-builder to retire. One of the best ways to curb our regret-builder and stop maintaining or building those ugly green things is to bring a bright light into our life. These monsters do not like light, they are nocturnal, they prefer to hide in the shadows of our thoughts and light is the only way to rid us of these nasty pests. We can bring a bright light into our life by realizing, by remembering that we are mortal. By being aware of the fact that this could be our last day; the day we move on, the day we move off of life's grid, this could be the day we die.

Do we want to waste, waste what little time we may have left in this life? In what may be our last day, our last hour and our last moment building, maintaining, and feeding these ugly green, nasty, time-consuming monsters. Do we want to keep feeding these regrets, regrets about something that happen yesterday, something we can never, ever change? Do we? It is non-reversible.

It is a big waste of time!

There's absolutely no use in regretting. We cannot change anything. Our mother died, our father died, our spouse died, or a child died. We cannot change anything. If someone you loved died, ask yourself: if they would want you to build an ugly, green regret in their memory. Build a memorial-regret over their passing and then feed that regret for the rest of your life. Alternatively, would they want you to take a short time to grieve and then move on, move on with your life and live out the rest of it in peace? If they loved you, really, really loved you, I am sure they would have chosen the latter.

Deaths and other incidents from your past

cannot change. All that was yesterday is yesterday; it is the past, it is behind us, it is beyond us, and we can never, ever go back. So why regret? We might as well regret about missing out on finding treasure, missing out on riding in a space shuttle or missing out on going to the moon.

Building regrets is a non-productive activity and a significant waste of time, time in this life that is so limited. With regret maintenance, we end up losing time, wasting time, time that will never return. Time is not something to waste if our time is limited and our time is limited. So why would we want to spend our precious time, our limited life regretting? We need to leave the past behind and start living in the present; it is all we have. It is the only way.

Another great way of avoiding building new regrets and dissolving current ones is with math. Yes! Math! In math, we have fraction and fractions have numerators and denominators. Using our life's actions as the numerator and our up and coming demise with the knowledge of not knowing when it will arise, as our Common Denominator.

"Remembering that I'll be dead soon is the most important tool I've ever encountered to help me make the big choices in life. "Don't let the noise of others' opinions drown out your own inner voice."

Steve Jobs 1955-2011

Our

Common

Denominator

Sorrow & Regret

Regrets & Sorrows

Sorrow & Regret

Regrets & Sorrows

Sorrow & Regret

Regrets & Sorrows

Chapter Seven

Our Common Denominator

PLANS
Make Your Plans,
But Keep in Mind
That You Can Die
At Any Time

The poem "Plans" reminds us that death is always at hand, always ready to reach out and shake our hand. We may make our plans for today, tomorrow, next week or next year, but we need to remember that all those plans, trips and reservations we make today, are tentative. They may never come to fruition. We need to remember too that all our plans are tentative; all life is a temporary affair as well.

One of the best ways to remember our tentativeness and understand the relationship between life and death is with math. In math, we have fractions and fractions have numerators and denominators. If we use our life's actions as our numerator and our impermanence as our common denominator and divide our numerator: our life, into our denominator: the fact that we are all going to die one day. All the people we know and don't know, our friends, our family, our pets and our-self are all going to die one day. We'll see that all human beings, all sentient beings have the same denominator. This common denominator is the fact that we are all mortal we will not live forever, and most of us do not know when we'll lose life's fire and thereby expire.

The fact that we can die at any time and any place should make us realize that our death needs to be our common denominator in life.

Since we are going to die one day and we do not know what day, death will come calling. Maybe next year, maybe next week, maybe tomorrow, or maybe later today it'll collect us. Take us away from all our accumulations, away from everything we've gathered, collected, and cherished; everything we've come to know and love.

•

WINTER WONDERLAND

Life is like snow; it only last so long, and we are snowmen in this: Winter Wonderland; every morning watching the sunrise, hoping today's temperature will not go above freezing. However, knowing one day it will. One-day spring will arrive; the crocuses, the tulips, and all the other spring flowers will bloom. Winter will be over; the snow will melt, and return again to water: the basis for all life.

•

In life: we need to use our impending death as our common denominator and everything we do in life as our numerator and divide our personal numerator by our common denominator. That sum, the result of that calculation would be that our life would begin to change. It'll start to lighten up as we realize: we do not have to cling to everything, attach ourselves to everything, and identify with everything around us anymore. Moreover, call that living since, like us, everything in and around us is impermanent. We'll soon notice that: we do not have as much time in this life as we thought. Since we could lose everything: our position-in-life, all our possessions, and all the people we cherish: our family, our friends and all our acquaintances at any time.

The fact that we could die at any time and everyone we know could die at any time too like all the other people who have died before us. Also, knowing one day we'll follow in their footsteps.

·

FOLLOWERS

One Day We'll Follow the Dead
From The Moment We Expire
To The Coffin, We'll Require,
To The Cemetery Where, We're Buried
With A Headstone at Our Head,
A Mound Over Our Final Bed.
Next to the Other Dead

•

If we use our imminent demise as our Common Denominator in life, we will soon see how minor everything we do in life is. Not insignificant in its self. However, irrelevant to our overall existence, to the fact that we will leave it all behind one day, on the day we die, and our demise could arise with the next sunrise.

Remembering that we only have this moment and this moment alone to live, love and be happy. Thus realizing each moment has its reward; our next moment is tentative, and this is the same for you, for me and for everyone we know.

Using math, in this way, is a great way of waking up to our mortality thus waking up to our fleeting moments, to our brief and temporary existence.

Me

&

My Coffin

•

My Coffin

&

Me

THE SURPRISE

A lot of people woke up yesterday

Not expecting to die yesterday

Where they surprised!

Me & My
Coffin

•

My Coffin
& Me

Chapter Eight

Waking Up at the Wake

A CORPSE IN A COFFIN

A Corpse in A Coffin
It's Our Future You See
A Corpse in A Coffin
One Day We Will Be
A Corpse in A Coffin
You & Me

Funerals aka Wakes! We have all been to

numerous Wakes aka funerals over the years, and they have evoked various emotions, a deceased spouse, a departed friend, a departed neighbor, an uncle, an aunt, mom, and dad. Most of us have been to quite a few over, the years and they've evoked grief, sadness and sometimes regret. We feel regret because we tell ourselves that we should've had more time with the deceased. We never told them how much we cared about them, love them and how much we are going to miss them after they are gone.

The deceased is gone, and we will not be telling them anything ever again, and they are never, ever coming back. In time, we'll forget about them if we do not turn on our regret-builder and start feeding it. Start creating little green monsters, little green regrets relating to the departed, regrets that may haunt us for years.

Our life will go on, go on until it is our time, our turn to be called the deceased and be the guest-of-honor at our own, our very own Wake and lie there with nothing to say. Just lie there with no speech to give and no hands to shake, lie there silent, still, stiff and cold. Exactly like all the other corpses, at all the other Wakes we attended; where people walked past the coffin, thinking the same thoughts we once thought when we attended a Wake. Some attendees will be sad, others happy, some indifferent, while some just come for the meal, still others looking forward, anticipating their financial reward from the decease's estate.

Are Wakes only for releasing our emotions about the deceased, getting a free meal or collecting cash from their estate?

Wakes can be a perfect place for waking ourselves up, for waking ourselves up to the fragility and the impermanence of life. It is a great place for looking at impermanence and seeing Impermanence-in-Action.

Impermanence-in-Action: the metamorphic change, the changing of a so-called permanent and living sentient being into a dead empty shell, a shell void of life, an inanimate object: a corpse, a carcass, a decomposing organism.

It is a great place for looking at our future and seeing how much more time in this life we may or may not have left. To realize one day, we will have no future, no past, and no present; our future ended, our clock stopped.

At a Wake, do you look in the coffin, at the deceased and only see the corpse, only see your previous relationship with it? Well, there is more to see, there is a lot more, a whole lot more to see: one can come away from a Wake, awaken, enlighten.

Enlightenment -a lightening up- can come from seeing the deceased in their coffin and realizing we are looking at our future. We are looking at what lays ahead, what lies down the road for us all. We are looking into tomorrow. We are looking at our real future, a future that will come to fruition for most of us when we least expect it and for all of us in the end. We need to realize that one day we'll be there too, a cold and silent, still and stiff corpse in a beautiful new coffin. A coffin surrounded by dozens of sweet smelling flowers, numerous notes of condolences, a long line of tearful mourners and, of course, those expecting an enormous bounty at the end of the wake.

Everyone needs to realize too: that they could be ready to be fitted for their new and shiny, humorous wooden overcoat tomorrow.

MY COFFIN

My Coffin & Me

When Will We Meet?

Is It Still in The Forest?

Or Displayed

On The Next Street?

It is hard to believe, but it is true since most of us have no idea when our demise will arise. It could be later today, tomorrow, next week or maybe next year, we just don't know. We hope our death will be years away, but it could be only hours, minutes or even seconds away. Tick Tock, Tick, Tock, Tick Tock. How many more Ticks, how many more Tocks do we have left, on our clock?

The time is now! Now's the time! To wake-up, to wake-up before it is our Wake, wake up before we are lying in our coffin at our very own Wake. The sooner we wake up to the realization that we only have this moment; the here and now and only this moment, no more, no less and see that we need to wake up now. We need to see that our clock is ticking; our time in this world is slowly slipping away with each passing day.

We need to become conscious of the fact that we could be the guest of honor at the next Wake we attend. Realizing that our Wake could be tomorrow thereby leaving everything we've accumulated: our family, our friends, our possessions, our position-in-life, and everything we treasure, behind.

WORRIED?

Worried About Losing Everything?

DON'T!

One Day Everything Will Lose You

Do You Have Plans?

Make Your Plans

But Keep in Mind

That You Can Die

At Any Time

Death Ed. 101

Chapter Nine

Naked Out

When it is time for us to leave, time for us to go, to strip down, to leave behind our inner and outer garb and get naked again. Will we be ready? When that time arrives, for us to return home, to the home we originated from and thereby returning to our original state of mind. When it is time for us to go back, go back home, go back to the land of nonexistence. Will we be ready?

A SIMPLE GAME

Life's A Simple Game
There Are No Winners
There Are No Losers
Everyone Comes Away from It,
Like They Came into It:
Naked

LIFE: NAKED IN; NAKED OUT

If we were born some time ago, and we've accumulated lots of stuff, now's the time to strip down. Time to let it all go, release it all, release everything, everything we've collected. Detach all of it from our psyche and clean out our ego.

Now's the time to get naked again, to let go of life's inveiglements before life lets go of us.

Now's the time to start embracing life, enjoying our family, our friends and forgiving our enemies, thereby remembering that this day, any day could be our final day to run and play, to sing and dance and enjoy the day.

So now's the time to strip away, to release all our accumulations, our baggage and get naked again. Now's the time to be ready to say: goodbye, ciao, adios to this life, this reality, this world.

We forget we have a non-refundable, non-changeable ticket for our flight through life, and our return trip is approaching. Are we ready for that journey, the return trip that takes us back to the land of nonexistence?

We need to remember too that like us, everyone we know and love and every other sentient being on this planet have the same return trip ticket. We all have the same type of boarding pass; a pass that doesn't allow any baggage; carry-on or checked. All of us are in a boarding line waiting for our next flight. Some will board today, some tomorrow, still others next week, next month, or in the coming years. But all will board the direct flight eventually and return to the land of nonexistence.

We need to check our regret-chest and see if we're ready, ready to go. Is it empty or is it full? If our regret-chest is full, full of regret material, the material we're feeding or material just waiting to be fed or fed again, waiting to grow then we better get busy cleaning it out. Before it has a chance to come to fruition again. We won't have time on the day we depart this life, and that departure could happen at any time. So do you have a lot of luggage or will you be traveling lite? The next flight to the land of nonexistence could take-off at any time, and there are very high baggage fees to pay before the flight departs even though no baggage is allowed on the flight.

We'll all die naked, ego-less, stripped of our positions, our possessions, our family, our friends and all of our other stuff, whether we like it or not. No one will be coming with us, no one; we'll make that last journey alone. They'll all be left behind to grieve over our passing or enjoy the treasures we left behind. All the treasures we accumulated throughout our life. All that stuff we thought we needed, all that stuff we spent most of our life gathering, and defending. It'll all be stripped away when we say our last goodbye. It'll be all sweep away when we reach our final animation point and become naked again.

On that last day, do we want that stripping away of everything we've attached ourselves to, to be painless or painful? The choice is ours. We need to make it now before it is too, too late; to make it before we are naked again.

LIFE: NAKED IN; NAKED OUT

THE ADVANTAGE

Animals have these advantages over man: they never hear the clock strike, they die without any idea of death, they have no theologians to instruct them, their last moments are not disturbed by unwelcome and unpleasant ceremonies, their funerals cost them nothing, and no one starts lawsuits over their wills.

Voltaire, philosopher and writer (1694-1778)

Me & My
Coffin

My Coffin
& Me

CAN YOU HEAR WHAT
DEATH IS ASKING YOU?
Why Do You
Cling, Cling, Cling
To Impermanent
Things, Things, Things?
Remember: When My Bell
Rings, Rings, Rings
You'll Lose
Everything, Thing, Thing...

Seize

the

Day

Chapter Ten

Seize the Day

Seize; Seize The Day

There's A Coffin

Heading Your Way

It May Arrive

Later Today

Seize; Seize The Day

How much of today are you seizing? All of it or just bits and pieces? Are you letting go of life, before it lets go of you? The only way to Seize the Day is to let go of its trappings, to let go of its hold on you and pull the ripcord and release it all. The more you let go of life's appurtenances, the easier it'll be to Seize the Day.

What would you do if you only had a year, a week, or a day to live? If you only had a year, a month, a week or a day to live, wouldn't you start seizing the moment, the day, the month, the year, right now? What makes you think you do not have only a year, a month or a day to live?

Just because you were alive, all day yesterday does not mean you'll be alive all day today or tomorrow. Your demise could arise with this sunrise or the next. Now is the time to enjoy the sun and appreciate the day because a sunset may not come your way if this is the day death comes by and says: Hi!

Seize today, tomorrow may not be a seize-able day.

OUR FINAL DAY

We May Only Have Today

So Let's Seize, Seize The Day

Tomorrow Who Can Say?

It Won't Be Our Final Day

•

Enjoy The Day While It Last

Before It Turns into Your Past

Enjoy The Day; Run & Play

Cuz It Could Be Your Final Day

•

Seize

the

Day

Chapter Eleven

Thinkable Things

UFO's

Recently a UFO (unidentified falling object) aka comet, meteor, asteroid crashed in Russia. The week before a much bigger one just missed the earth; a week after the Russian UFO incident another asteroid came super close to our planet. One struck the moon recently too. We see comets flashing across the sky all the time. What does it mean? It means we have to be ready, ready to discard our shell and leave this life at a moment's notice, because we may be closer to our end, to the end then we think.

Nobody died in the Russian UFO incident; they were all very lucky, but if it occurred over a populated area it would've been a lot worse, it would've been devastating.

How long will it be before the next UFO impacts the earth? Nobody knows when or how big the next one might be or when it'll make contact with this little ball we call home, make contact with our friends and family, with everybody we know and love. Nobody knows!

The Russian incident stunned and surprised all of us. It woke us up. We started to realize how small and vulnerable we all are and how close we are to death and destruction from the alien UFOs over our heads, in outer space, every day.

If we were in a UFO's path, we would, more than likely, have less a half-hour notice from NASA before it impacted the Earth and we were consumed by it. Not much time to do anything but pray.

Solar Storms

Don't get too dependent on your smartphone. Back in 2012, the Sun erupted with one of its most powerful solar storms ever. A solar storm that just missed the Earth but if it did hit was big enough to "knock modern civilization back to the 18th century," NASA said. However, few Earthlings had any idea what was going on.

"If the eruption had occurred only a week earlier, Earth would have been in the line of fire," said Daniel Baker, professor of atmospheric and space physics at the University of Colorado.

"I had come away from our recent studies more convinced than ever that Earth and its inhabitants were incredibly fortunate that the 2012 eruption happened when it did," said Baker.

If the 2012 solar storm could have taken us back to the 18th century, it means that solar storm could have knocked out all the computers on this planet. Everything would have stopped: from our washing machines to our smartphones. It could've caused all cars to stop dead on the roadways and more than likely it would have taken out all communications and computers on all autos, trucks and aircraft.

The damage would've been in the trillions, and there would be mass starvation since our modern style of living requires refrigeration and transportation to function. Moreover, we missed it all by just one week, but just because we missed this one it does not mean we'll miss the next one. It is just another reason to be ready, to be prepared and not surprise since we do not know if the cause of our demise will come from the earth or the sky when it does arise.

We were lucky again, but will we be next time?

Which only proves again that we have to be ready and not surprise when our death arrives. We have to be ready for our final day, be prepared, for our last moment on our departure day. Prepared because our demise could arise not just from a condition within us, around us, or below us, but from something unknown, in the outer space above us.

• BE PREPARED & NOT SURPRISE •
• WHEN DEATH ARRIVES •

Impermanent Being
CLINGING
Impermanent Things

ARE YOU?

An
Impermanent Being
CLINGING
Impermanent Things

Impermanent Being

CLINGING

Impermanent Things

ARE WE?

Impermanent Being

CLINGING

Impermanent Things

Chapter Twelve

Expiration Dates

PLANS
Make Your Plans
But Keep In Mind
That You Can Die
At Any Time

If you do any driving and shopping, then you are concerned about parking meter's expiring time and food expiration dates.

If you are concerned about what you eat, then you are concern about a food's expiration date. How much time it as left before it is unusable and ready for the trash. Expiration dates are on almost everything perishable: milk, cheese, veggies, and meat.

The one thing we hardly ever place an expiration date, though it has one, is on oneself or any of the other people we know or don't know. Sometimes, doctors, do issue expiration dates when they say someone has only x number of days, weeks or months to live and he/she cannot postpone their demise any longer than that date.

We humans and all the other sentient beings living on this ball are perishable, we all have expiration dates though most of them are not known. Knowing we all have an expiration date and will expire one day is an excellent way to remember we are in the same boat and are only travelers, passing through this life. All of us are just visitors, guest with departure dates, expiration dates, and anything collected in this lifetime, any of our baggage from this world will have to be left behind when death calls and says no more time; You are expired!

Two excellent ways to remember that we are just impermanent beings with no need to cling is with expiration times and dates. Take parking meters they are great timepieces to focusing on impermanence. What is more impermanent than time, we see it changing all the time it is never permanent. The clock never stops.

When we park our car and feed the parking meter, and the meter food is consumed by the clock as it ticks away and has to be feed again if we want more parking time.

Parking meters and expiration dates on foods are excellent tools for understanding and focusing on our impermanence and so is the simple poem below: Plans.

PLANS
Make Your Plans
But Keep in Mind
That You Can Die
At Any Time

The poem ends with the statement: "you can die at any time." there is no truer statement ever made.

If we keep that point in mind, the point that our life could end at any time, it could end in the coming week, in the next hour, in the next 10 minutes, we just don't know. If we remember our mortality and the fact that all of us are impermanent beings, and our demise could arise at any time could lead us to an uncontaminated, wholesome, moment to moment life. Two of the best ways to keep that point in focus is with expiring times and expiration dates.

• Parking Meters: They are Expiring Time Machines aka clocks. With parking meters: when we feed the meter for an hour or two and leave, then think about the poem's last line "you can die at any time" and wonder if we'll return to feed that meter again, or come back to pick up our car. Will our time run out, expire before the parking meter's time expires? It probability will not but the possibility is there, and it is an excellent way to remember our mortality.

• Food: Another great way to focus on our mortality is with food. Food has expiration dates. When you are shopping and are checking expiration dates on food and want to concentrate on the impermanence of self and how quickly one's life could end then look at the time on the food's expiration date stamp and wonder who will expire first, the food item you are buying or you. More than likely it will be the food item, but the possibility of it being you is always there. Remembering the last line of the poem: you can die at any time.

PLANS

Make Your Plans

But Keep in Mind

That You Can Die

At Any Time

Chapter Thirteen

The Pseudo Death Experience (PDE)

The Pseudo Death Experience PDE is part of a "well-dying" trend that caught on in South Korea. Many in South Korea, who participate in a PDE, seek relief from the stresses of modern life. Today there is current tension, especially among young South Koreans, over highly competitive college entrance exams, job searches, long working hours and widening inequality.

PDE's attracts over 15,000 participants a year ranging from middle school students to elderly people who want to know what their deaths will be like and how to prepare for the end of their lives. A PDE helps the participants map out better futures.

It is a business very similar to a massage studio, but unlike massage studios that have massage tables, a PDE studio has coffins.

In South Korea, their PDE starts in a dimly-lit room filled with dozens of coffins where people dressed in white burial shrouds sit down next to the coffins.

Before they climbed into their coffins, they listened to a lecture on life and death, write their Will, then lie down. A symbolic "angel of death" - a person wearing a traditional Korean hat and black robe - goes around and closes the lid of each coffin.

After about 10 minutes they slowly sit up inside the wooden coffins. Some blinking, pale and solemn, they say they thought about their past and their dead parents, spouses, children, friends, and neighbors while inside the caskets.

Others feel sad, feel sorry (to their family) that

they did not do anything on anniversaries, holidays and missed their children's parties and other events. Some choke with tears.

Most gained courage, and vow to live better, more fruitful, lives after the experience.

A CORPSE IN A COFFIN

A Corpse in A Coffin
It's Our Future You See
A Corpse in A Coffin
One Day We Will Be
A Corpse in A Coffin
You & Me

A CORPSE IN A COFFIN

A Corpse in A Coffin
It's Our Future You See
A Corpse in A Coffin
One Day We Will Be
A Corpse in A Coffin
You & Me

USING A PDE

• One way of using a PDE is if we want to see what it might be like being dead. We could connect with what life is now, with its events, ones missed because we postponed them and one's completed. It could be a good time to check our bucket list. What do we want to do before we die and are we moving towards that goal?

• Another way of using a PDE is to look at the impermanence of life and the permanence of death from the perspective of a corpse in a coffin.

• With a PDE we could see what we'll lose when our form ceases to perform, and the lid is closed in our coffin. It is a great time to look up at that closed lid and see what value, our possessions have to us.

• A PDE may help if when we go to a Wake and look at the deceased in their coffin and wonder what it would be thinking if it could be thinking or what did it think before it stopped thinking. If it had unfinished business or regrets about what it missed or could or should have done before their book of life closed. What flashed before him/her during the last moments of their life?

• A PDE may help If you ever wondered what your final thoughts might be when death come by and says Hi and you say goodbye.

• PDE is a good place to work on big and small social, economical, and overall attachments. A great place to see how all of those issues only relate to you if your outside of your coffin and are meaningless to you when your inside your coffin.

DOING A PDE

Where do I go for a PDE?

You could go to South Korea, and that would be very expensive for a 10-30-minute session, or you can save money and do it in the safety of your home, alone, or with a mate or trusted friend.

How do I do a PDE?

1.Doing a PDE is easy. It is something you can do at home alone or with a friend. All you need is a clean white sheet big enough to cover you from head to foot, a timer, pen and paper and a comfortable place to lie down.

2.Find a safe place to lie down (a hard surface works best) Dress as light and be as comfortable as possible, remove your shoes, take out your pen and paper and write a Will then set the timer for 5 minutes.

•• For Couples: just follow steps one, and two then continue. Lay down and imagine you are being placed in a coffin, and then let the other person put the sheet over you starting at your feet and slowly moving toward your head and stopping at the neck. Pausing for a few seconds and then slowly covering the head. As this is being done monitor yourself, and if it gets to be too uncomfortable then stop, pull back the sheet and continue it later. The experience should last for about 10 minutes per session. As you lie, there think about life and how you are living it, what you might regret if you were a corpse in a coffin. During that time monitoring yourself and if it gets too uncomfortable then fold back the sheet from your head and stop. Continue it later if you wish. Your first experience may only last a short time.

•• For Singles: just follow steps one, and two then continue. Lay down and put a folded sheet at your feet. As you lay down, imagine you are being placed in a casket.

Pull the sheet over you starting at your feet and slowly moving toward your head and stopping at the neck. Pausing for a few seconds and then slowly covering the head. Keep covered for 5 minutes. As you lie think about life and what you would regret if you were dead. During that time monitoring yourself and if it gets too uncomfortable then fold back the sheet from your head and stop.

Like any other exercise, it takes time. Your first try may only last a few seconds, and that's ok. Continue it another time. The more you practice, the easier and longer your sessions will be.

A DEPRECIATING ASSET

A Depreciating Asset

That's You & Me

Our Value Is Decreasing

As Our Life Moves

Toward Ceasing

EPILOGUE

A DEPRECIATING ASSET
A Depreciating Asset
That's You & Me
Our Value Is Decreasing
As Our Life Moves Toward Ceasing

After reading the poem "A Depreciating Asset,"

some ask why: Why would our value be decreasing as our life moves toward ceasing?

The people who ask that believe there is only one significant value in life: monetary value and that value increases as their bank account grows. Those folks are not looking at the big picture. Their monetary value, their dollar value, is minute compared to their limited-time, their life-value. Most people forget that their time, the time remaining in this world, on this planet, in this life for them -their real value, their life-value- is decreasing and it decreases, loses value with each sunset, with each passing day as they grow older and older; their life moves toward ceasing.

Today we have one less day of life left than we did yesterday and tomorrow, today will be another lost day of our life. Our life-value is decreasing with each passing day as our life moves toward ceasing.

Our life is like a very fragile bag, a bag filled with a limited number of balls. Each ball, a day of life in that bag, a bag that can burst at any time and release its contents into space, a bag filled with balls and each ball a day of our life. Every 24 hours one ball slips out of the bag and disappears into space. Another day lost and the value of our bag of balls, the value of our life, our life-value decreases as our life moves closer and closer to ceasing.

We mustn't forget if the ball-bag is damaged or emptied by time and all of its contents are gone, the bag (our life) becomes valueless. We become just another empty shell, an empty unusable bag of bones, a bag to be disposed of, a corpse ready for the 3 B's, ready to be bagged, boxed then buried and then soon forgotten.

Life's 3 B's

One day we'll all be just another cold and stiff corpse, a form that stopped performing, a body that will need to be collected and then disposed of by another. A corpse that's ready for the 3 B's; a body that's ready to bag, box and bury or burned. Moreover, as a corpse our bagging – placing us into a black plastic body bag for transport- will be the first "B". The bagging is the first thing they do to us when they collect us from our L.A.P. (last animation point) aka point of death. The point where we will lose all our production value, all our titles, our accolades, and our relationships with everybody and everything we knew and loved in this world. Everything, we held on so dearly to, so tightly to, everything around us will be released when our plug's pulled, and we are disconnected from this life. At that time, we'll lose most of our value in life, except for some monetary value to the boxing center aka mortuary and sentimental value to our friends and family.

Once at the boxing center, we'll lose our first "B", our black body bag and then prepared for our second "B" our boxing. It is a place where we are made ready, dressed up and placed in a box aka coffin. The coffin then put on display in an exhibition room at the boxing center aka mortuary; our body will be lying there for the last time in its shiny new coffin.

It is all being made ready for us to be the guest of honor at our last Wake. Just lying forever silent surrounded by dozens of sweet smelling flowers, notes of condolences and a long line of tearful mourners, including our family, our siblings, our peers, our friends and maybe some enemies too. Some of who will be estimating their share of our estate once the last "B" completed.

Once on display, our sentimental value will increase, and this value will level off, till its time to seal the box, to seal our coffin. At that time, our sentimental value will jump and peak, and then remain steady until it is time for our last "B", our burial. Once in the ground, our sentimental value will start dissipating as everybody goes to our After the Wake Dinner.

Chicken or Beef!

As time rolls on, we will be forgotten, and any value we had will disappear altogether.

In Time

In time, we'll be alone and valueless.

In time, we'll be forgotten like all the others who were unremembered before us.

In time, we'll be just another empty shell on life's beach, just another empty shell in a box, under a stone in a cemetery.

Just & Another Stone

A Cure for the Fear of Death

Perhaps the best cure for the fear of death is to reflect that life has a beginning as well as an end. There was a time when you were not: that gives us no concern. Why then should it trouble us that a time will come when we shall cease to be? To die is only to be as we were before we were born. –

William Hazlitt, essayist (1778-1830)

Just

Another

Stone

JUST ANOTHER STONE

One Day We'll Be

Just Another Stone

Sitting On the Lawn

Next to Other Stones

Of People Who Believed,

Believed They Belonged,

But Now Are All Gone

FEAR

"I do not fear death. I had been dead for billions and billions of years before I was born, and had not suffered the slightest inconvenience from it."

Mark Twain   (1835-1910)

"We, the bones that are here, await yours." (Unknown)

ON LOAN

If, every day, I dare to remember that I am here on loan, that this house, this hillside, these minutes are all leased to me, not given, I will never despair. Despair is for those who expect to live forever. I no longer do.

Erica Jong, writer (b. 1942)

A Part Of Life

DEATH

"Death is a part of all our lives. Whether we like it or not, it is bound to happen. Instead of avoiding thinking about  *it, it's better to understand its meaning. We all have the same body, the same human flesh, and therefore we will all die. There is a big difference, of course, between natural death and accidental death, but basically death will come sooner or later. If from the beginning your attitude is 'Yes, death is part of our lives,' then it may be easier to face."*

Dalai Lama (1935-)

A
Part
Of
Life

FRIENDS

Old friends pass away, new friends appear.
It is just like the days; an old day passes, a
new day arrives. The important thing is to
make it meaningful: a meaningful friend -
or a meaningful day.

Dalai Lama (1935-)

You Won't

Need

Your Purse

In

Your Hearse

ANATOMY OF GREED

A Greedy Man/Women on Life:
MORE, MORE, MORE, MORE ...

A Greedy Man/Women on Death:
NO, NO, NO, NO ...

A Greedy Man/Women Dies:
No more, no more, no more, no ...

Greedy Men & Women at Rest: Forever More

"A REMINDER"

You Won't Need Your Purse
In Your Hearse

A Final Note

IT'S TIME

Now's The Time
To Keep in Mind:
One Day You're
Going Off Line
Your Connection
Will Be Severed
You'll Be Out
Of This Life
Forever

This Disconnect
Will Happen
To Most of Us
When We
Least Expect It
And to All Of Us
In The End.
Our Limited Time
Our Limited Life
Will Come to Its End

DEATH

Death can Happen

at Any Time:

In the Morning

In the Afternoon

At Dinnertime

DEATH: Our Mentor, Our Muse

Death: the mentor, the motivator for us to reprioritize: our goals, our relationships, our life.
Death: the realization that shows us, we only have this moment, this day, this life.
Death: the appreciator, that reminds us to be happy, to embrace and enjoy life while we can, cause we're in a very short life span.
All three remind us to appreciate this moment, this day, this time. It's all we have and will ever have. We all need to remember there is no more, but there will soon be less.

notes

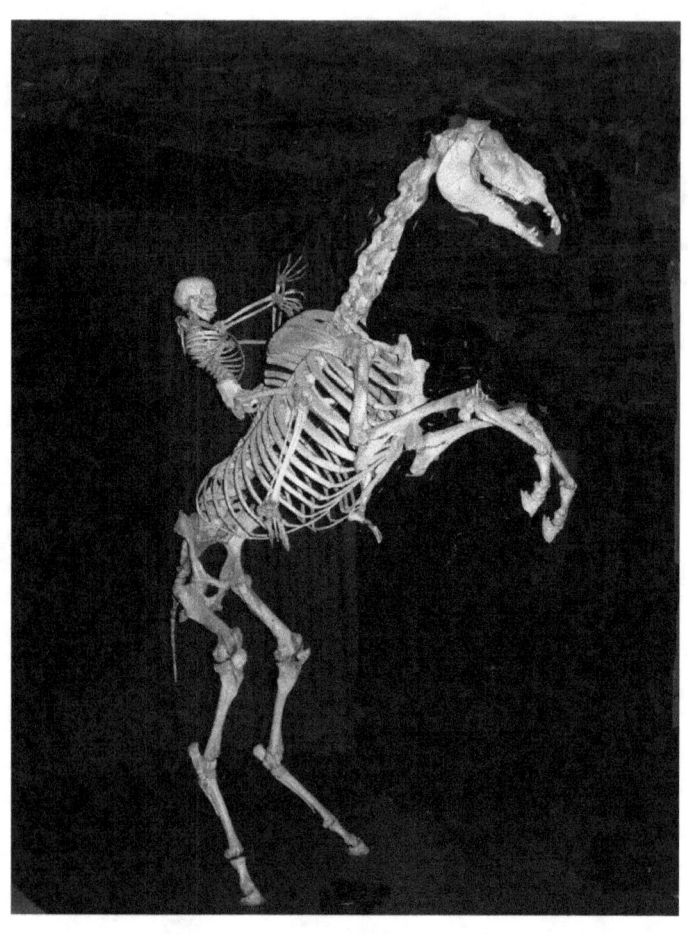

ARE YOU MAKING PLANS?
Make Your Plans,
But Keep in Mind
That You Can Die
At Any Time

notes

notes

notes

Visit us at:

www.deathhappenstoo.com

Death Ed. 101